OTTERS

First published in Great Britain in 1994 by
Colin Baxter Photography Ltd.,
Grantown-on-Spey,
Moray PH26 3NA
Scotland

Reprinted 1997

British Library Cataloguing in Publication Data
Tulloch, Bobby
    Otters
    I. Title
    599.74447

    ISBN 0-948661-44-5

Photographs by:

Front Cover © Laurie Campbell (NHPA)
Back Cover © Laurie Campbell
Page 19 © Bridget Wheeler (Survival Anglia)
Page 20 © Laurie Campbell
Page 21 © Laurie Campbell
Page 22 © R Hare
Page 23 © Colin Baxter
Page 24 © Allan Potts
Page 25 © Geoff du Feu (Planet Earth Pictures)
Page 26 © Nick Gordon (Survival Anglia)
Page 27 © Nick Gordon (Survival Anglia)
Page 28 © Bobby Tulloch
Page 29 © Laurie Campbell
Page 30 © Laurie Campbell
Page 35 © J Watkins (FLPA)

Page 36 © Laurie Campbell
Page 37 top © Laurie Campbell
Page 37 bottom © J MacPherson (Scotland in Focus)
Page 38 © R Hare
Page 39 © Charlie Hamilton James (Plant Earth Pictures)
Page 40 © R Hare
Page 41 top © Bobby Tulloch
Page 41 bottom © Bobby Tulloch
Page 42 top © Bobby Tulloch
Page 42 bottom © Laurie Campbell
Page 43 © Bobby Tulloch
Page 44 © R Hare
Page 45 © Charlie Hamilton James (Plant Earth Pictures)
Page 46 © Laurie Campbell (NHPA)

Otter Illustration by Keith Brockie

Printed in Hong Kong

OTTERS

Bobby Tulloch

Colin Baxter Photography Ltd., Grantown-on-Spey, Scotland

K. Brockie 93

Otters

I was born and spent my childhood on a croft on the east side of the island of Yell in Shetland. Our house was only a hundred yards or so from the rocky shoreline where much of my childhood time was spent – apart from the unwelcome necessity of having to go to school.

Pounded by the south-easterly storms in winter, or calm and tranquil during long summer evenings, the sea and shores were a never-ending source of interest and amusement to me as a small boy. This interest was accentuated by the fact that I was raised during wartime when luxuries such as conventional toys were entirely unobtainable. Even the fish we learned to catch made a welcome addition to the meagre rations we were allowed to buy from the local shop. Looking back, it is obvious that we did suffer some deprivation, but I am sure we also gained a lot of self reliance, and learned to make or adapt much of what we needed.

I suppose I would have been about five or six years old when one day at my usual pastime of poking around in rock pools while the tide was out, I became aware of a large cat perched on a seaweed-covered rock nearby. It was chewing at the remains of a fish of some kind and I was puzzled at its appearance. Our local cats used to spend time hunting on the shores, some even learning the trick of taking young saithe out of a rock pool with a deft flick of a paw, so seeing a cat eating a fish on the shore came as no surprise. But this cat was like no other I knew. It had a dark-brown coat which looked all spiky and wet. When I called out 'puss puss!' to my amazement and some alarm, it instantly dived off the rock into the sea, never to re-appear.

When I later told the story to my parents, they laughed at me and explained that what I had seen was an otter. This incident sparked off what has been a lifelong interest in this most charismatic of all British wild animals.

All otters are members of the family *Mustelidae* which in Britain includes the Stoat, Weasel, Pine Marten and Polecat. The family is characterised by having long, lithe, muscular bodies, strong, thick necks, short legs and a fairly long often bushy tail. All are carnivorous, preying on other animals or insects. Stoats and Weasels live mainly at ground level while Polecats and Pine Martens are arboreal to a degree. Otters are aquatic and live alongside lakes, rivers or seashores, living mainly on fish, crustaceans and other aquatic creatures. They are excellent swimmers and divers.

There are (usually) nine species of otters recognised in the world, divided into three tribes. The *Lutrini* tribe, to which our own Eurasian Otter *Lutra lutra* belongs, has three species, the American River Otter *Lutra Canadensis* and the Sea Cat *Lutra felina* of South America are the other two. The tribe *Anoychini* has five species ranging from South America through to India and Burma, and include the 'true' Sea Otter *Enhydra lutris* of the Alaskan coasts. The tribe *Hydrictis* has only one species, the Spotted-Necked Otter *Hydrictis maculicollis* of Africa.

The Eurasian Otter formerly ranged over much of Europe and Asia from Great Britain in the west to Japan in the east, and from northern Finland to northern Africa and even Indonesia. But in many places, due to hunting pressures, destruction or pollution of habitat, otters have become either extinct or much reduced in numbers. In Britain the decline of the otter can be legitimately blamed on persecution by men in one form or another. Otter hunting with hounds became fashionable in England as far back as the Elizabethan era and continued with varying degrees of intensity until as recently as the 1970s, by which time there were so few otters left in the traditional hunting rivers that many people became alarmed by the decline.

Pressure groups began to lobby for the protection of otters and by 1978 legislation was passed giving complete protection to otters in England and Wales. This still left Scottish otters unprotected, and fears were expressed the the otter hunts would turn their attentions north. In fact one or two tentative attempts were made to establish hunts in south-west Scotland, causing considerable local opposition. However, the establishment of the Wildlife and Countryside Act in 1982 clarified the situation and gave protection to otters over the whole country. Not only are the animals themselves protected but it is an offence to wilfully disturb the breeding dens (holts) of otters.

The pressure from otter hunting, although contributory, is however unlikely to have caused the catastrophic decline in otter populations, particularly in the lowland areas of their habitat. The more sinister threat from the increased use of pesticides and herbicides, especially of the persistent DDT types used in crop sprays and the increased water pollution from leakages or deliberate dumping of industrial chemicals containing mercury or PCBs (polychlorinated biphenyls), are more likely to have caused otter decline. These poisonous chemicals find their way into the watercourses and the food chain, and build up in otters from the fish on which they feed.

Another problem which faces the otter is the increased tendency of water authorities to 'tidy-up' river banks, which makes them more like canals, and destroys the riverside trees among whose roots otters traditionally make their holts. And as if all this isn't enough to discourage otters, there are also the increasing leisure activities of the expanding human population which discourages animals from using many of their traditional haunts.

In the face of all this pressure, *Lutra lutra* has become more or less confined to the wilder, less populated parts of the country. Upland hill streams in some parts of Wales and the West Country still have scattered populations, and they are fairly widespread in Ireland. However, the only parts of the country – indeed of Europe – where otters can be said to be still common are the remote rivers and coasts of north and west Scotland, and especially the outer isles. It often comes as a surprise to people accustomed to thinking of otters as essentially river animals to find that in places like Shetland, in the absence of rivers, the animals have become very well adapted to making their living from the sea.

Otters are quite large animals; adults are between three and four feet (.9 - 1.2 m) in length, males being the largest. There are stories of old dog otters of over five feet (1.52 m) in length recorded. Males weigh up to 25 lb (11.3 kg) and females about 16 lbs (7.3 kg). They are dark-brown in colour when wet, but this changes markedly as the animal dries out, some appearing almost ginger. I know of one family which consistently produces individuals which are fawn in colour. As in most animals, albino forms occur from time to time, and otters with white patches are not uncommon. There is always a paler area around the face and bib and this varies with the individual. The wet fur is reflective and otters have an uncanny ability to take on the shades of their surroundings. There is one feature which is of great help in identifying individual otters; these are the variable lip and throat patches which are almost white and appear to be peculiar to each individual.

Otters have little or no subcutaneous fat, so they depend on their thick fur to keep out the cold. This is very different from seals, who have only a thin coat of hair and depend for their insulation on the thick layer of blubber beneath the skin. An otter's tail is muscular and tapers to the end; it is used in manoeuvring under water, and in fact is often called its 'rudder'. An otter's foot has five toes joined by partial webs, and it is useful to remember this when you find a trail of footprints across the sand at low tide. To avoid any confusion between dog and otter tracks, remember that a dog has four toes on each foot and a medium dog's footprint is about the same size as an otter's, although the webs don't show up on sand; the mark of five toes should remove any doubts.

There is (and may remain) some mystery as to how otters came to Shetland in the first place. Shetland is separated by nearly a hundred miles of sea from the mainland of Scotland and although there are 'stepping-stones' in the form of the Orkneys and Fair Isle, this still leaves a minimum of 25 miles of open sea. I find it difficult to believe that an otter could swim that distance without its fur becoming waterlogged. So, could the otter claim to be Shetland's only indigenous mammal? Could it have swum across in the post-glacial period before the sea-gap became so large? I suppose it is not impossible, but I am inclined to think our population stemmed from either escaped pets (even the Vikings were known to keep otters as pets) or unwitting stowaways. Otters are extremely inquisitive animals and are known to investigate boats regularly (they use mine as a 'sprainting' place). They have been known to hide in lockers or under floorboards when disturbed, and with boats calling at different ports they could easily have been transported in this fashion.

Otters are resilient animals, masters of the art of concealment and quick to adapt to changing circumstances. While otters have a wide appeal to people, *Lutra lutra* has always been difficult to study in the wild, and much of what has been written and shown is as a result of studies on other otter species. My own knowledge of 'river otters' is gleaned entirely from what has been written about them, but it is essentially the same animal (in spite of assertions that we have 'sea otters' in Shetland). My contact with coastal otters spans many years here on Shetland. Over time I have come to know many otters personally and learned much about their fascinating life cycle. The following account of one of my local otter families is the story of a typical year in the life of an otter.

* * *

The three animals lay entwined in an 'ottery tangle', the only movement came from their gentle breathing. They were asleep, but a sleep never far below conciousness, the slightest sound would be enough to make three pairs of eyes snap open immediately, to assess any present danger. The mother and her two young are deep in a jumble of boulders which forms the breakwater for the landing ramp of the car-ferry pier. This particular section of coast is rather short of ready-made holts, and otters are not very good at extensive earth working. So the previous spring the pregnant female was quite pleased to find that the digging machine, which scared the daylights out of her at first, had gone away leaving a fine jumble of boulders, which after avoiding for a week, she carefully examined one dark night. The smells of men were all around, but she learned

9

to accept this as part of the normal environment, and because of her approaching confinement, saw the advantages of a ready-made birthing place.

She had worked out the ferry timings fairly quickly, and during the quiet time collected the soft heads of the tangles (seaweed) which waved their fronds in the tide, and used them to line the cavity under the boulders where she would give birth. The dog otter took no part in these proceedings, he had other business to attend to because in the 10 kilometres of coastline he controls and patrols, he has no less than three females in his harem, two of which are pregnant, including our female.

The two cubs were born in late May, tiny helpless creatures whose only instincts were to search for the nipples from which came their life-giving milk. In more southern climes it is thought that female otters come into season at any time of the year, but my observations in Shetland lead me to believe that there is a more definite season here and that after a nine week pregnancy, most cubs are born in spring, usually late May or early June.

The cubs grew slowly as the summer progressed, their mother rarely left them at first, except to grab a quick feed of butterfish or sea-scorpion. The cubs' eyes opened when they were about a month old and they began to peer myopically around the confines of their den. At seven or eight weeks they were little fat bundles of fur, and could totter on stubby legs. The instincts to play and bite each other became apparent and their mother decided it was time for a bit of house training. She had already been giving the youngsters bits of half-chewed fish, so their droppings were more noticeably fishy and she encouraged the pair, a dog and a bitch, to go out to the entrance of the holt to defaecate.

At about three months old the mother decided the time had come to introduce the cubs to the element in which they would spend much of their life – the sea. They were reluctant to enter the water at first, especially the little female, and their mother was not above nudging them off a slippery rock where they had no choice but to fall into the sea. They would then come paddling back urgently to dry land, whimpering their little high pitched squeaking whistles. She also began to catch small fish and give them to the young cubs to kill; the crevices of the breakwater had plenty of eelpout, butterfish, young lumpsuckers and sea scorpion, which were not difficult to handle.

The cubs treated it all as a game, though their mother knew instinctively that it was important training for the time, not too far away, when they would have to find and catch all their own food. As the cubs' confidence grew, they ventured farther afield with their mother on hunting trips. Sometimes mum would catch a fish, but instead of giving it to the cubs she would let it loose in a rock pool. The youngsters would then have to chase and catch it with a great deal of splashing and tussling over who should get the prize. This taught them to put their heads under the water, because, of course, there is still one major skill they have yet to acquire and that is to learn how to dive.

Up to now the cubs had merely 'dog-paddled' after their mother, their well-fed little bodies were quite buoyant in the water. But now at about three months old they were more like small versions of their mother, if a little tubbier. When she thought they were ready, the mother swam with the cubs out into deeper water, then first one then the other were grabbed by the scruff of the neck and taken down a few feet under the water before being released. They didn't like this at first and would immediately head for the shore, squeaking furiously, but instinctively they came to realise that this was to be their normal habitat, and that here their bodies could move faster and with more agility. Above all, here were fish and crabs to be caught.

So, by the time the days began to shorten, when the crops on land were ripened, and when the sea and all its creatures were at their most prolific, the otter family wandered far away from the holt in which they were born. They used a number of daytime holts scattered along the coast where they could lie up and sleep off a meal, and had several encounters with a large dog otter who tried to be friendly, but was furiously chased off by the mother with much spitting and whickering. Although the cubs probably didn't know it, this was their own father whose attentions were less than welcome.

There was much for the otter cubs to learn; the daily hunt for food was largely routine, they learned to follow their mother down among the waving kelp beds where the rocklings, sea scorpions and big slow-moving lumpsuckers lived. Small items were often eaten while swimming on the surface and they soon found that they could hold a fish between their front paws to prevent its escape. Occasionally, big fish were found by the cubs, but they were still not strong enough to deal with them effectively, and mother usually stepped in to deliver the *coup-de-grace* and bring big powerful species such as conger or ling ashore on to the rocks or the beach to let the cubs squabble over who got the best bits. The female cub, although smaller than her brother, made up in determination what she lacked in size and often came off best.

Mother brought ashore a large octopus one day and the cubs took on quite a sticky problem before they were able to subdue it. The octopus fought valiantly, wrapping its tentacles around the legs of the cubs as it tried desperately to get back into the sea. But the small teeth of an otter cub are needle sharp and the octopus was dismembered in a few minutes. Crabs are numerous among the seaweed and because they tried to run away they were teased by the cubs unmercifully. Sometimes it wasn't entirely one-sided and a big crab could hang onto a cub's nose until it bled. Occasionally when other food was not immediately available crabs were eaten, but it is not a preferred food.

The cubs learned to obey warning signals from their mother and would stay motionless until danger passed. The shepherd and his dog, who regularly patrolled the coastline, were given due respect. The collie dog in particular was not to be trusted, having a frightening propensity for rushing up and barking at the otter family. The shepherd always called his dog off, mindful of stories of encounters between otters and sheepdogs where the dog had come off worst.

Other animals which called for some respect were seals, and the otters were wary of them while in the water. If a seal became too curious and approached closely, the otters made for the rocks and waited ashore until the seal had gone away. Great Black-backed Gulls were an irritation rather than a problem. These all-seeing opportunists kept a sharp eye on the activities of the otter family in the hope of picking up left-over scraps of fish. They were not above swooping silently near to one of the cubs while it was eating a fish, then suddenly giving a loud squawk. As often as not, the startled cub would drop its meal and rush into the sea, whereupon the gull would pick up the fish and fly away. A variation of this trick is played by Hooded Crows, who fly up silently behind the otter while it is chewing away and stabs the otter on the back with its beak. Even the mother otter was caught out by this trick on occasion and the crow got a meal.

Sometimes, for a change, the mother would take her cubs up one of the small streams which flowed into the sea. Here they would chase and catch small eels and young trout until satisfied, then after a good roll around on the heather to dry off, they would curl-up and go to sleep under the shelter of the bank. On coasts where otters are not often disturbed, they will often sleep for hours curled up on the seaweed or on the rocks in full sunlight.

The family had suffered no serious mishaps and now at the year's end, they were back in the familiar surroundings of the holt where they had been born, hearing without alarm the thump of the car-ferry as it docked, the voices of the people and the engines of the cars as they drove on up the hill.

* * *

Otters and man live in reasonable harmony in the crofting areas, where they are generally liked and respected. Not too long ago, however, they were seen as a legitimate part of the produce of the land. An otter skin could be sold for a sum which could keep a crofter's family in food for a week or more, so in Shetland at least, otters were hunted wherever they occurred in sufficient numbers.

Most districts had a noted otter hunter who made part of his living from shooting or trapping otters, and there are many tales of the exploits of these men. One of the methods of trapping otters was by so-called otter-houses. These were small stone built enclosures about six feet in length by a couple of feet high and wide – literally a tunnel of stones. These were built over known otter runs or paths, and were constructed with a wooden drop door at the entrance which was held in the open position by a string. The other end of the string was trapped by a pivoting stone on the floor which, when stepped on by the otter, released the string so that the door dropped down and trapped the animal inside. Although this practise is no longer legal, in some remote areas the remains of otter-houses can still be seen.

One tale which has become part of the folklore of the Shetland Islands concerns a man who hunted otters, called Robbie o' the Glen. One day, as Robbie made his customary round of his otter traps, he found an animal caught inside. He lifted one of the roof stones and felled the otter in the usual way, then gripping his prize by the tail, he slung it over his shoulder and set off home. At some point on the journey the otter, which had only been stunned, came to life and Robbie found himself 'gripped by the tail'. Neither was prepared to give up its hold on the other until Robbie, no doubt in agony, cried out "Let be for let be!" and each let go.

Another story concerns an otter-hunter who lived on the island of Fetlar. He had a tame female otter which he kept in his barn. It was free to come and go through a glig (flap) in the door, and at the right season she would often attract a male otter to come courting. As was usual in the old days, the barn was built next to the living room and any noises from the barn would be heard through the connecting door. So, when the man heard sounds which indicated that his otter had a visitor, he would sneak outside and close the glig. Then, taking his flail, he would go into the barn and fell the visiting otter. In this manner he got many a good skin to sell.

One night he heard a great commotion coming from the barn, so after closing the exit, he seized his flail and went through the door. In the barn he found not one but several dog otters competing for the favours of his female. The man laid about him with the flail in great excitement, and when all had been subdued he found to his horror that he had also killed his own beloved otter, and by so doing also killed his 'Golden Goose'. He was said never to have killed another otter for as long as he lived.

As a boy I well remember our local otter-hunter. His name was Willie Thompson but he was known simply as 'Shootin' Willie' because he was hardly ever seen without his 12-bore shotgun over his shoulder. He not only hunted, but he studied otter behaviour and had a knowledge of the subject which would be the envy of many modern naturalists. His hunting method was shooting rather than trapping, and I heard of an incident which was similar, though slightly more serious, than that suffered by Robbie o' the Glen. Willie had shot an otter quite near a cliff edge not far from Gossabrough where he lived, and, like Robbie, had slung the otter over his shoulder to carry home. Again the animal, having only been stunned, came to life and sank its teeth into Willie's back. Willie's reaction was to fling himself down on top of the otter and attempt to get at the knife he habitually carried. In the ensuing struggle the pair of them rolled over the cliff edge and fell some distance. But Willie came off best and managed to get his knife out and dispatch the otter. But he didn't get off lightly and spent several weeks in bed recovering from the damage inflicted by the fall — and the otter's teeth.

Since the Wildlife and Countryside Act became universally applied and otters have enjoyed the protection of the law, there have been noticeable changes in otter behaviour. Several generations of otters have now had no reason to live in fear of mankind, and there does seem to have been a significant response. They have become less nocturnal in their behaviour, and have begun to make use of sheds, barns and the like, even for breeding.

However, the recent harmony between otters and mankind has not been entirely without problems. There have been a number of reported cases of otter predation on livestock in Shetland. These attacks are usually directed at ducks or chickens, but cases of the killing of geese and even turkeys have been reported. The recent development of salmon farming in the islands and the north of Scotland, however, presents a more serious area of conflict for otters.

As most farms are in typical and traditional otter (and seal) habitat, there are obvious potential problems. Young fish are reared in large net enclosures placed in sheltered sea inlets or 'sounds' between islands. Each net may hold several thousand salmon, and is supported by a buoyant frame, which also supports the walkways from which the salmon are fed and tended. The temptation of having, within their territory, cages full of delicious food must be fairly irresistible to an otter, and although anti-predator nets are a planning requirement, otters are resourceful animals when it comes to fish. Undoubtedly many otters have paid the penalty for their inquisitiveness, and reports of large amounts of salmon being lost through holes chewed in the protective nets by otters does not help their cause. Locally, one or two persistent offenders have been live-trapped by the more enlightened and sympathetic farmers and transported well away from the farms to another part of the island.

Because of my known interest and sympathy for the otters, I may not always be told the true story, but I believe many salmon farmers now realise that otters are attracted to the cages not so much for the salmon but for the other fish, such as saithe, which gather round the salmon cages to take advantage of spilled and surplus feed. Local salmon farmers have described how they have been feeding their salmon from the floating walkways between the cages while an otter has been catching saithe nearby, and eating them on the same walkway.

It is frequently claimed that otters are wasteful eaters and cases are cited where the observer (often a fisherman) has come across a salmon or trout on the bank of a river with only a single bite taken out of it. Personally I am sceptical about the claim. I have watched hundreds of otters eat a meal and am often amazed at just how much fish an otter can eat at a sitting. I have yet to see an animal take a bite or two and then *voluntarily* go away and leave it. It is much more likely that the otter was disturbed, probably by the approaching observer, and has slipped away unseen. Otters may have rather limited eyesight in some ways, but there is nothing wrong with their other senses.

Salmon farming is not the only development to affect the continued well-being of local otter populations. North Sea oil was discovered back in the 1970s and it was decided to pump the oil ashore to Orkney and Shetland through pipelines. From shore-based storage tanks the oil would then be loaded into huge oil-tankers for distribution to the world's markets. The possibility of an oil spill became very real indeed, and only weeks after the oil started flowing it became a reality. An empty tanker berthed at Sullom Voe, the large oil terminal in Shetland, accidentally bumped one of the mooring piers and split a hole in its side. Unfortunately the hole was in one of its fuel tanks, and over a thousand tons of oil spilled into the harbour. Oil recovery systems which were still at the development stage proved entirely useless, and the oil escaped from the immediate area and polluted miles of rocky coastline. This coastline supported a healthy otter population and sadly over twenty corpses were collected on the shores. But how many actually died and were not recovered will never be known.

One oiled female which was found alive (but later died) was lactating, and a cub, which probably belonged to her, was picked up and taken home by a friend of mine who was a commercial fisherman. It was given little preferential treatment over the dogs, cats and children already in the household, except that it was regularly provided with fish. The little otter was not confined and became just like one of the family, and was even put outside with the cats at bedtime.

Eventually it began to stray away from home for longer periods, and established a holt in a drainage ditch near a fresh-water loch not far from the house. But the neighbours began to report that chickens were going missing and suspected that the otter was the culprit. So a live-trap was constructed and set in a hen-house, and sure enough, the otter walked into it and was caught red-handed.

Of the options considered deportation seemed to be the kindest, and as I had a boat and was not too far from several uninhabited offshore islands, I was invited to organise the operation. The offending animal was brought over (still in the catching box) and we took it out to the chosen island which was about a mile offshore. The otter was released and given a feed of fish, and while it wasn't looking we sneaked off and came back to the harbour feeling that it was a job well done, and a satisfactory solution to the problem. About ten days later the true but sad end to the story came to light. A crofter at the other end of the island (about 16 miles away) went out to feed his chickens one morning, and when he opened the hen-house door he found an otter asleep on a heap of chicken feathers. Closing the door quietly he went to the house for his gun and returned to kill our rescued otter.

Following the Sullom Voe oil spill, and in the expectation that it might not be the last, an otter sanctuary was established by a lady who had suitable facilities in the north mainland of Shetland. While a trickle of waifs and strays of the otter kind have passed through her hands in recent years, it was not until the winter of 1993 and the grounding of the tanker *Braer,* with the loss of 85,000 tons of oil at the southern tip of Shetland, that a major oiling incident appeared imminent.

But while the wind, blowing to hurricane force at the time, drove the helpless tanker on to the rocks, it also seemed to disperse the light quality oil amazingly quickly, so that it didn't get a chance to build up along the shoreline, So this, coupled with the fact that the area is sparsely populated by otters, meant that only a few animals were known to have died in the incident. But this proved that we shouldn't live in a fool's paradise. For even though Shetland is located far from the more polluted parts of the industrialised world, our wildlife populations are by no means safe, especially from the effects of the never-ending quest for cheap forms of energy.

Otters living near the sea usually have little problem in finding fish
to eat. Sloping rocky shores often have dense kelp beds in which small fish
can shelter and breed. Being expert divers and swimmers, otters are
quick to exploit this handy food source.

An otter likes to find a meal without spending too much
time under water. It prefers to hunt in water of only two or three
metres depth, each dive lasting about half a minute.

From a distance one otter looks much like another, but most
have pale spots or blotches on the lip or throat. These can help to identify
individuals, as no two otters have the same markings.

On the surface otters swim with a 'dog-paddle' movement,
but under water the body becomes sinuous and graceful. Forward
movement is aided by the strong muscular tail.

Small fish are often eaten at the surface, with the
otter sometimes holding the fish between its paws. Larger
prey are usually taken to the shore to be eaten.

Otter Watching

Luck has a big part to play in otter watching – probably more so than most British mammals. One of the main reasons for this lies in the unobtrusive and stealthy nature of the animal. I have little experience of riverine otters, but it would seem that they are particularly elusive. I would expect this to be the result of pressures of disturbances of one kind or another. But even where otters are under little or no pressure, they still tend to maintain a low profile. Luck has been expressed as 'being in the right place at the right time', and if that is so then you can influence your luck by some knowledge and planning.

Perhaps you are visiting the seaside and wonder what the chances are of seeing otters. If you are at a popular holiday resort with lots of people and perhaps dogs, you can probably forget it. But if you are on an island (not too far offshore) or near a remote sea-loch, say in the west or north of Scotland, then your chances begin to be realistic. The thinly populated crofting counties are probably best, and the first thing I would do would be to ask locally; bring up the subject perhaps in the local pub, and with luck you will be regaled with stories of encounters with otters. Just as in the old days when most districts had an otter hunter, so it is now that there is usually someone in an area who knows otters. *That* is the person to get on to.

Okay, you have been advised of a section of coastline frequented by otters; how do you set about getting a glimpse of the elusive beastie? I am sorry to say, but the least likely way is to organise a family party which may include children and dogs. It is much better to go alone, or perhaps as a couple who stay close together and speak quietly. It is also an advantage to dress unobtrusively. I am convinced that otters have a dislike of red. One cub I was raising by hand was even scared of a dish of tomatoes, and a little girl who came to see it wearing red welly boots, was disappointed when the otter refused to come out from under the couch, and sat as far back as possible spitting furiously.

Otters appear a bit myopic, and they certainly have a limited perception of still objects, but they seem to have an acute visual memory for anything new in their territory. This applies particularly to outlines, so it is a good idea, once you have spotted an otter, perhaps fishing a little way offshore, to get down under a bank or behind a boulder, so that you are not silhouetted against the sky.

If possible choose a calm day, or at least one with light winds; this not only increases your chances of seeing an otter's head in the water, but it could also mean that your scent is not carried to the animal. The best coastline for seeing otters is unlikely to contain predominantly high cliffs or extensive sandy beaches. Neither of these are much used by otters. High cliffs are likely to have deep water into the cliff base and otters prefer the easier living in shallow water. Wide, sandy beaches, on the other hand, have a limited range of available food and probably the adverse psychological effect of making the animal feel conspicuous.

An otter's ideal stretch of coastline will have mainly low rocky shores with perhaps a few small, shingly or sandy beaches. It should be backed up either by peaty or uncultivated grassy hillsides, and ideally should have one or more small streams entering the sea. A gently sloping hinterland usually indicates a similar underwater profile for some distance out from the shore. This provides the best habitat for kelp and other seaweeds, which in turn provides the best breeding grounds and cover for the small fish which are the staple food for otters. Rocky shores backed by earthy banks are also much favoured because they usually contain crevices, caves or holes in the peat which make good holts or daytime lie-ups.

Fresh-water streams are irresistible to otters. Not only are they a source of food such as eels and small trout, but overhanging banks offer concealment. Otters use streams as part of their territories and create an obvious pathway across an island, which avoids their having to cross open land.

At certain times of the season otters leave quite obvious signs of their passing – once you have got to know what to look for. The polite name given to otter droppings is spraints and they serve at least two purposes. The obvious one is to evacuate the bowels, and females and cubs will leave droppings wherever they need to, this may be on the seaweed on the shores or in the water. But males also use spraints as signals to other otters of territorial claims. These sprainting points are always on prominent rocks or on grass tussocks, and are an indication to other otters of who just passed this way. Spraints are usually rather dry and contain lots of small fish bones. Blackish at first, they dry out to a grey colour. Some fresh spraints have blobs of a jelly-like substance which is believed to be an information package to other otters. This possibly passes information such as the state of oestrous (breeding status) of females and other signals about which we know little. In Shetland these sprainting points are often established and most active during late winter when otters are busy defending territories and seeking mates, but are usually left to wither (and weather) in summer when there is less need for the dog otters to worry about rivals.

In your section of ideal shoreline there will be small promontories, noticeable shoreline rocks or gaps through fences or stone walls. These are the places to look for spraint points and they are often obvious from the brighter green colour of the vegetation caused by the nutrients contained in the droppings. Another place to find spraints is by the margins of small pools on the hillsides near the shore, and a breeding holt often has a mess of smelly spraints outside the entrance.

If initial examination of your chosen shoreline shows signs of sprainting activity then it is a question of walk and watch. I find that sitting down and just watching is a waste of time, it is better to walk along the shore, where possible staying off the skyline, and to keep a watch for an otter out fishing. They generally feed above the kelp beds where the water is not too deep, an average dive lasts between 30 seconds and (rarely) one minute. If the otter disappears beneath the surface and doesn't re-appear for *two* minutes, you have almost certainly missed seeing it surface to take a breath.

To get a closer look you should stay motionless while the animal is on the surface, then do a quick dash to a new vantage point when it dives — but don't chance more than half a minute. There is no animal of its size which can disappear more quickly or completely than an otter when it is aware of being watched.

The time of day is not too important where otters are undisturbed, though I think the first couple of hours after dawn are as good as any. Also, although I have seen otters at all states of the tide, the first half of the flood tide is a good time; then the rocklings and blennies are at their most active.

Patience, sharp eyes and luck is the recipe for the successful otter watcher. Happy hunting!

Following a feeding session, otters often spend some time grooming
their fur on the seaweed – and then curl up to sleep.

No rest for the dog. Back to work to catch more fish.

Otters are sociable animals and usually tolerant of each other –
although females with cubs can be a bit irritable.

Family groups often hunt together – and share the catch.

Coastal holts are often dug out of the peat,
but small handy caves are also used.

Otters like to keep a clean holt. They often form dung-heaps just outside the entrance which may contain many fish bones.

These cubs are about nine months old. They often hunt together
and then squabble over their share of the fish.

When a female otter has young she becomes very possessive,
and even the father of the cubs must keep away, or get attacked.
Cubs stay with their mother for up to a year before they wander
off to perhaps find a mate and set up their own territory.

Caring for Otters

Otter populations have been depressed for many years, due largely to pollution, destruction of habitat, persecution and disturbance from mankind. But it is perhaps the threat of pollution which poses the most alarming problem for both otters and humans. Residues of pesticides such as DDT, Aldrin and Dieldrin, along with other similar substances such as those known as polychlorinated biphenyls (PCBs) – and heavy metals like mercury, cadmium and lead – have all been found at worrying levels in otters. The presence of these chemicals have come from intentional dumping and 'leakages' and can have various effects: from immediate mortality in more localised spills, to as yet not fully understood, harmful long term effects in the aquatic food chain and habitat.

It is clear that otters need care and protection to survive and there are ways you can help them. Learning more about otters and getting involved in otter conservation is a beginning. Don't be afraid to ask questions on environmental issues. The more people who become aware of otter problems and are properly educated, the better. Agreement and stricter legislation on the control of pollutants is desperately needed on local, national and international levels. Water authorities, or anyone owning or responsible for a wetland area should be made aware of the importance of protecting the otter's natural habitat along rivers and shores, and encouraged not to clear and 'sanitise' them unnecessarily.

There are otter conservation groups around the country which you may wish to support by volunteering or by making donations, but choose carefully and find out how your money will be spent before making a contribution. When travelling through otter areas, drive carefully, otter road casualties are depressingly frequent. When watching otters or visiting their territory remember that while they do tolerate humans, you should be aware of not disturbing them unnecessarily – especially mothers with cubs. If you show respect not only for otters but also their habitat, your reward may well be the pleasure of spending time in the company of one of the country's most charismatic and elusive animals.

Otter Facts

Scientific Name: *Lutra Lutra* or European Otter

Average Length: Male 1.2 m Tail .45 m
(Scotland/UK) Female 1.0 m Tail .40 m
Newborn 12 cm

Average Weight: Male 8-10 kg
(Scotland/UK) Female 6-7 kg
One month old 7-800 g

Distribution: Formerly ranged over much of Europe and Asia, from Great Britain in the west, to Japan in the east, and from northern Finland south to northern Africa and even Indonesia. Their population suffered serious decline in the 1960s and have since become extinct in many areas or much reduced in number.

Reproduction: Female oestrus approximately 36 days. Breeding may take place at any time of year, though may be restricted in certain areas. Gestation lasts approximately 63 days with an average litter of two. Cubs' eyes open at about 30-35 days, and take solid food at two months. They learn to swim at about three months and stay with their mother until about 12 months old.

They are fully mature at about two years old. Average longevity not known, they suffer a high rate of early mortality, but in some cases may live to perhaps 10 or even 15 years.

Vocalisation: Various whistles, whickerings, twitterings, chitterings and when startled: 'Hah!'.

Recommended Reading: There are a few excellent books available which provide more detailed information. These include: *Otters* by P.R.F. Chanin, Whittet Books, 1993; *Otters: Ecology and Conservation*, C.F. Mason and S.M. Macdonald, CUP, 1986; *The Natural History of Otters*, Paul Chanin, Academic Press, 1985; *Track of the Wild Otter*, Hugh Miles, Colin Baxter Photography, 1989.

Biographical Note: Bobby Tulloch was born on Yell, Shetland's largest island, where he lived on his family croft. He was a naturalist of international reputation, with a passion for studying and photographing wildlife in the northern isles and around the world. He was a well-known lecturer, tour guide and author, and his life and work featured in television series such as *Naturewatch* and *The World About Us*. He died in 1996.